PRAISE FOR *BULLET POINTS*

"Jennifer Sutherland's book-length poem *Bullet Points* is relentless, harrowing, and tremendously smart. With uncommon acuity and force, Sutherland chronicles experiences of both public and intimate violence, writing back from trauma and toward something new and necessary. This book is an absolute accomplishment."
—NATALIE SHAPERO, author of *Popular Longing*

"A crucial addition to the literature, a sharp outline around a stopped heart. In *Bullet Points*, Jennifer Sutherland writes her way into the body that remains back there. It is meaningful to make art out of any day, but maybe especially a day like this one."
—PATRICIA LOCKWOOD, author of *Priestdaddy*

"*Bullet Points* is not merely a lyric; rather, it is a narrative of what happens when the space between 'victim' and 'witness' becomes collapsed. It is unflinching — an interrogation of both violence (particularly against women) and the retraumatizing nature of storytelling. Sutherland wields the precise imagery of a poet alongside the disciplined languaged of a lawyer, delivering us a profoundly necessary look into what we've allowed to be normalized in the United States. This is a story we need now."
—STEPHANIE LANE SUTTON, author of *Shiny Insect Sex*

"A book-length poem composed for the purpose of binding and banishing a trauma, and which successfully does so, is called a masterpiece. Read and participate in a banishing spell, sealed by the grit-in-your-kneecap-skin, up-and-running-again determination that compels Jennifer Sutherland's writing."
—EVE ETTINGER

bullet points

bullet points

A LYRIC / JENNIFER A SUTHERLAND

RIVER RIVER BOOKS
Durham, North Carolina

Published in the United States of America

Library of Congress Cataloging-in-Publication Data
Sutherland, Jennifer A, 1972–
Bullet Points: a lyric / Jennifer A Sutherland.
ISBN-13: 979-8-9881378-1-8
Subjects: LCSH: Gun Violence—Poetry. | LCGFT: Poetry.
Classification: LCC 023937888

Cover and interior design by Alban Fischer

RIVER RIVER BOOKS
10 Linganore Place
Durham, NC 27707

www.RiverRiverBooks.org

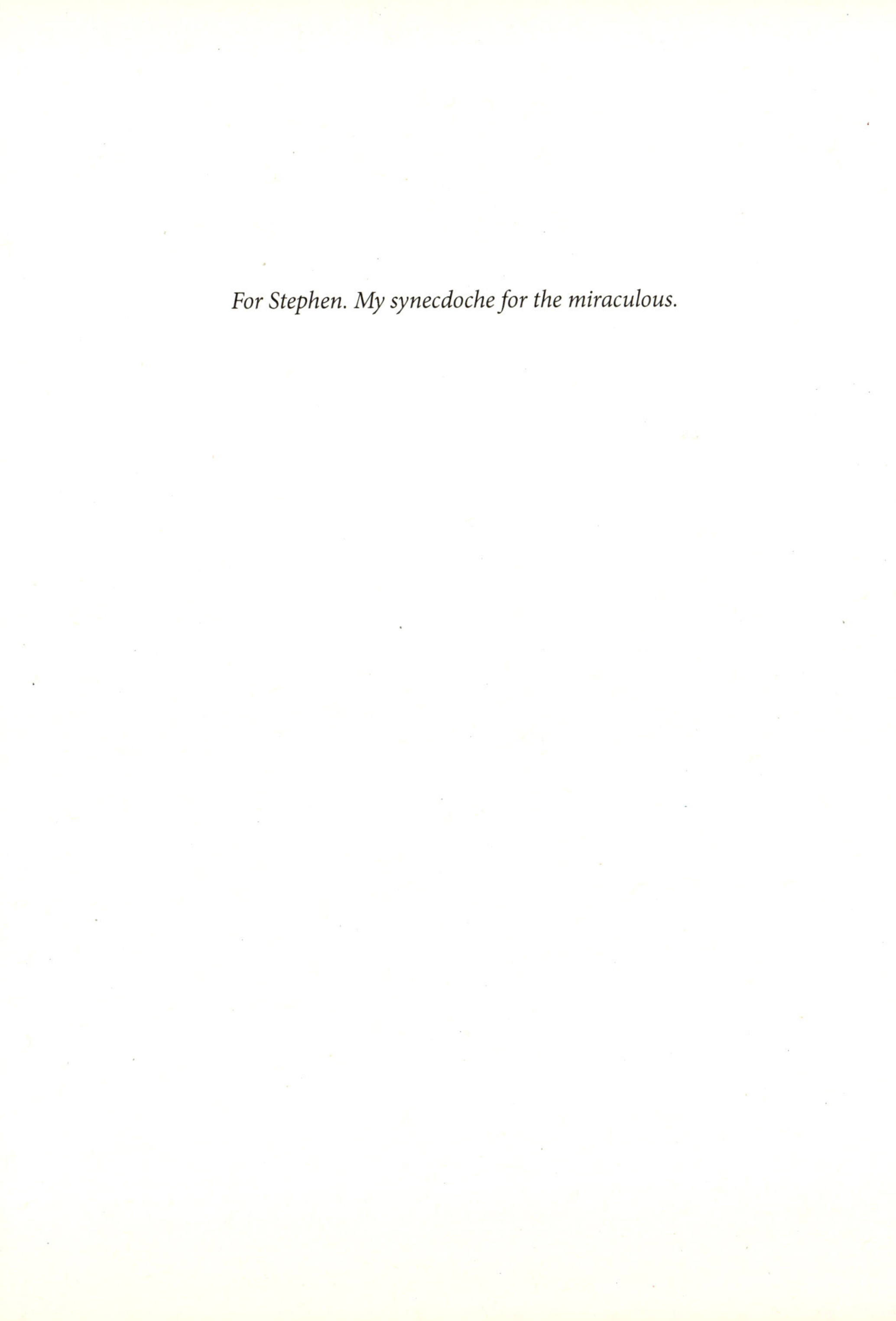

For Stephen. My synecdoche for the miraculous.

Dealing with you is a kind of dealing with Spirits, an Invisible Body subsisting only *in intelligentsia legis.*

—JOHN POLLOXFEN,
A Discourse of Trade, Coyn, and Paper Credit (1697)

I really believe the virtual world mirrors the physical world.

—MARISSA MAYER, *Vogue Magazine*, 2009

Early morning, February 11, 2013.

I recline upon the bed in my hotel room. Indolent woman. Noise of traffic in the street beneath. Noise from the television.

The world outside is bustling, moving like a market square, importing, exporting. I carry what happens next inside me like a balance sheet.

A man is filmed beneath a woman's skirts while she prepares to eat. Her skirts are wide, wide. She seats a country or an idea.

Policemen scurry by searching for him but her face is still. The fabric of her skirt lies close to the fire but doesn't catch.

I put on a pinstriped suit. The patterns on a fabric or a particular cut of clothing evolved to telegraph the wearer's status or their occupation.

Chaucer's Sergeant at the Law, for example, wore "a silken belt of pin-stripe stuff."

The women of the Enlightenment often wore the verdugado. Not a bustle, which is something different though it also carries space beside the body for the body to inhabit.

The name derives from the word "verdugo," meaning green wood. "Verdugado" now means "executioner" or "assassin."

A bullet fired into water transforms into a stone and sunlight follows from the entry point, becomes a path or tunnel. At the exit there is silt and sand, a mouth that swallows. A word that stills.

The verdugado is also called a farthingale. In the Ditchley portrait, Elizabethan skirts swell voraciously above all of Europe at her dainty feet.

"She can but does not take revenge" is written on the canvas beside her. Also: "In giving back she increases."

Language is one way of doing business across time and into spaces. Image is another.

One sinks its roots far down and waits. The other sends out shoots and colonizes.

I don't know which I prefer since both are dangerous. I focus on my voice instead, even if my speech is alien.

You might assume an octopus propels itself along by grasping with its tentacles but that assumption would be false. An octopus moves by internalizing and then expelling water.

An octopus is mostly water. An octopus is the basis for many creatures' founding myths: the Gorgons. The undulating Kraken.

Joan of Portugal popularized the verdugado when she wore one to hide her pregnant belly. Scandalous, as she did not bear her husband's child.

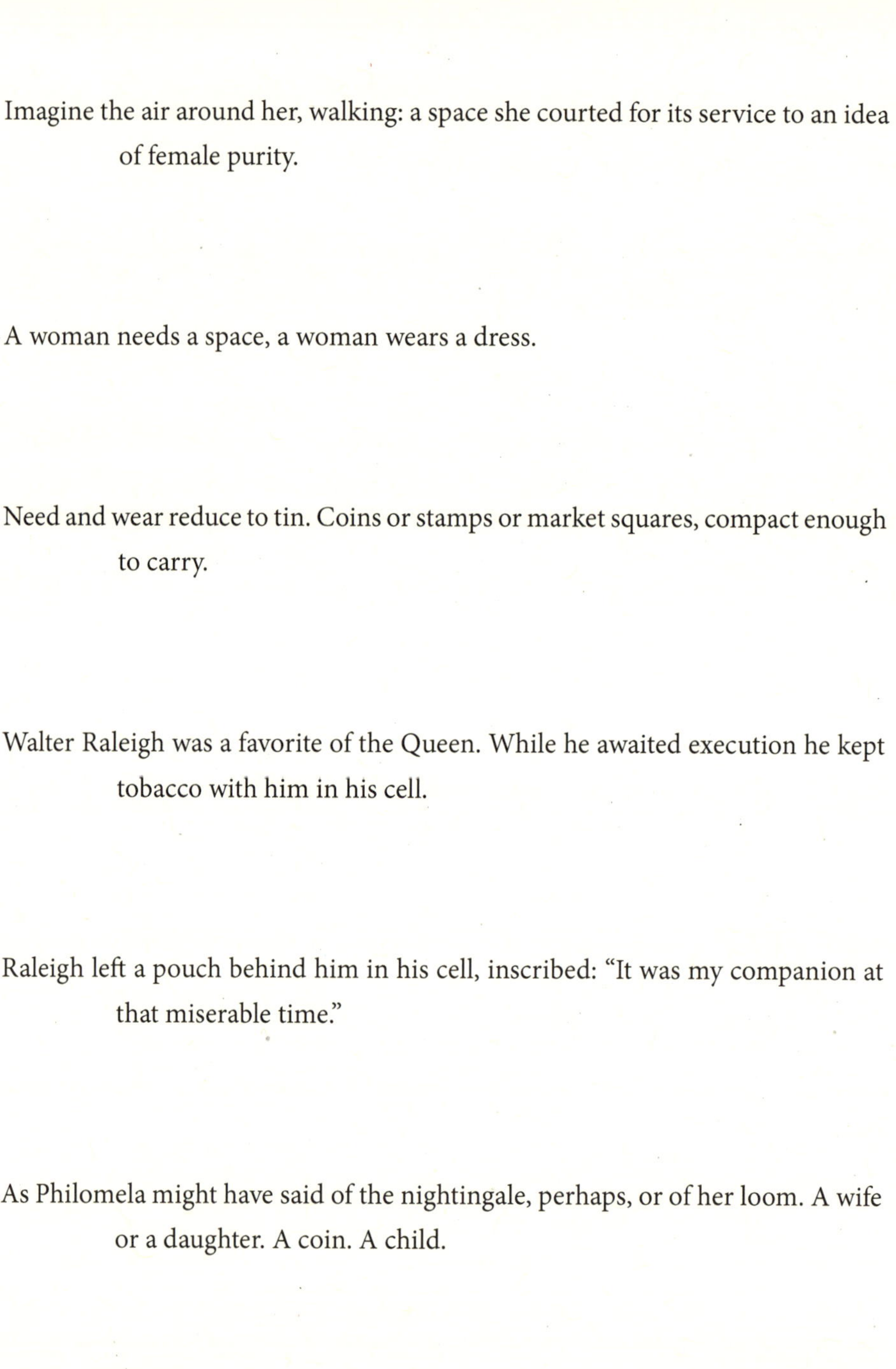

Imagine the air around her, walking: a space she courted for its service to an idea of female purity.

A woman needs a space, a woman wears a dress.

Need and wear reduce to tin. Coins or stamps or market squares, compact enough to carry.

Walter Raleigh was a favorite of the Queen. While he awaited execution he kept tobacco with him in his cell.

Raleigh left a pouch behind him in his cell, inscribed: "It was my companion at that miserable time."

As Philomela might have said of the nightingale, perhaps, or of her loom. A wife or a daughter. A coin. A child.

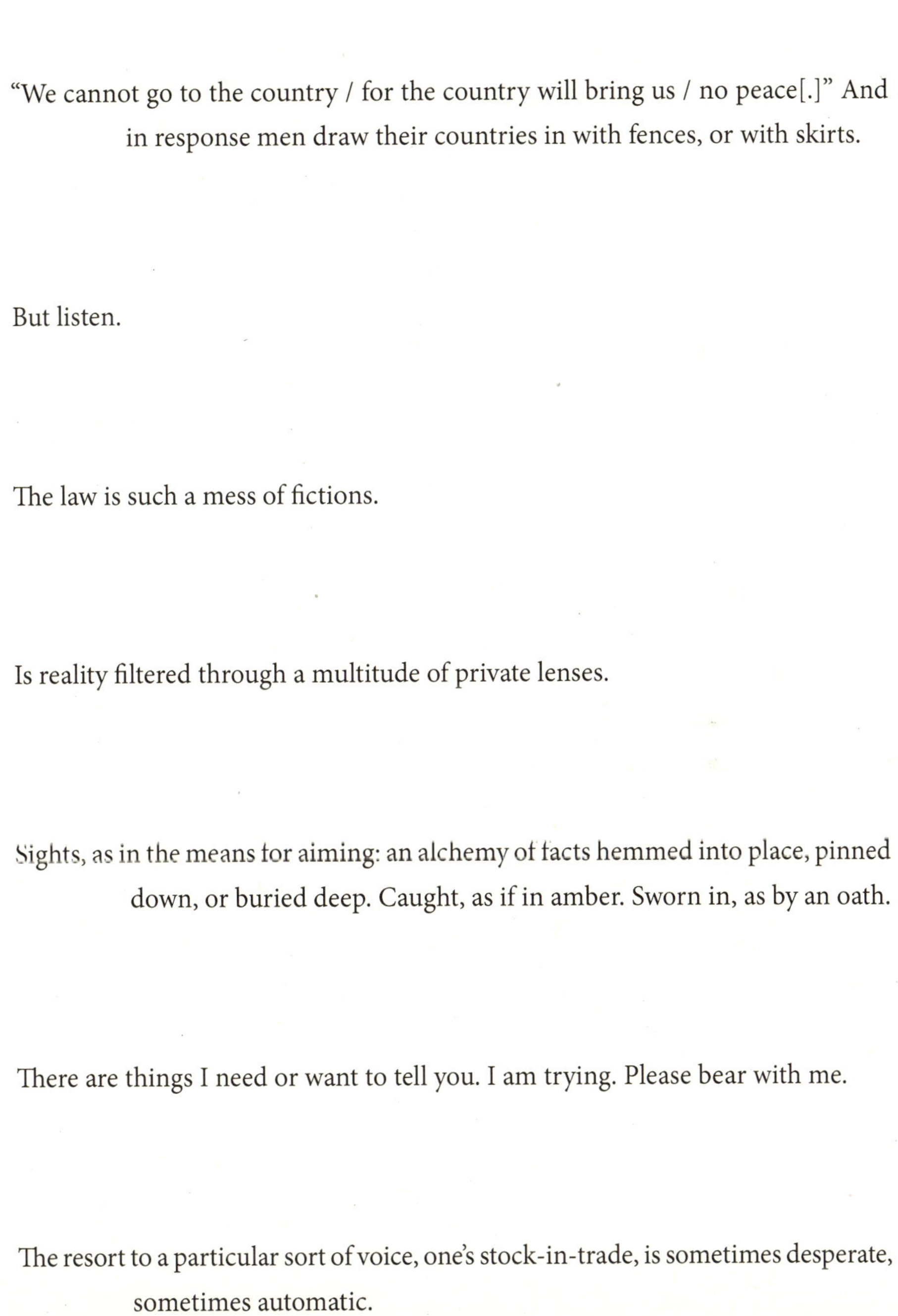

"We cannot go to the country / for the country will bring us / no peace[.]" And in response men draw their countries in with fences, or with skirts.

But listen.

The law is such a mess of fictions.

Is reality filtered through a multitude of private lenses.

Sights, as in the means for aiming: an alchemy of facts hemmed into place, pinned down, or buried deep. Caught, as if in amber. Sworn in, as by an oath.

There are things I need or want to tell you. I am trying. Please bear with me.

The resort to a particular sort of voice, one's stock-in-trade, is sometimes desperate, sometimes automatic.

It may indicate the body's systems of defense springing into action, or the mind's effort to escape, a detour around an occupier.

It may signify the modulation of a scream or cry, especially one that does not recognize itself. A tool employed cheaply, for attention perhaps. Or a test, like an air raid siren.

This has been a test of the emergency broadcast system: there, you see. It has only been a test. And then the voice collects itself and the narrative-as-itself continues.

The hotel room in Wilmington. The sunny winter morning.

My colleague calls to say he's in the parking lot. Let's call him H.

H. will drive me to the courthouse, where we will try our case before a judge who's famous for his corporate expertise.

Don't turn away or let the abstract frighten you. The story will embodify, but only when the space beneath the skirt is ready.

A famous poet told me why I could no longer speak as I had spoken before the shooting. "You're still there," she said to me, "in the stairwell. You can stay there, or you can leave."

Like an octopus we reach for what we want even when it reaches back into our mouths.

Travels lengths of nerve and bone. Explodes into blossom moving at the speed of pain.

I think of Charles Bovary. How Emma spends him into bankruptcy chasing things beyond her station. The village bailiff arrives one morning and then he carts it all away.

Everything, gone. The tablecloths, the mattresses, the hairbrushes, books, the doctor's own straight razor. Can you blame Emma for eating her own death then, after?

Would not any man have fed her poison were he in the doctor's place? There is precedent, of course.

"If you saw a bullet / hit a Bird — "

Metaphor is a kind of fiction. It propels a narrative by projecting it in or on another body. And the body carries on the business. It's a simple calculation.

But I digress. I tend to do this. To delay.

Once I took my children to a park. It was autumn, time for stories and for casting stones into moving water.

In the park there was a railway bridge, not old but built to seem that way, and beneath it flowed a shallow stream.

First we walked down to the water's edge. The children gathered stones and threw them, listening for the sound.

The sound told us when the stone had met the surface and then bored its way down.

Opening a long long hole into the water, to the silt and to the sand beneath.

We are creatures of our doings even when the doings sink us.

Then we walked up the embankment and stood upon the bridge. Jersey walls along each side, not high but made of concrete.

Meant to halt a wayward vehicle's momentum but not a person's because a trajectory is chosen.

I explained this to my oldest because he asked me why the Jersey walls weren't taller so that someone couldn't fall right off the bridge into the water (and here he made the pebble smacking water sound).

I told him people come up onto the bridge because they want the view and to be viewed. To see both down below and all around.

Why does the view matter, he asked, so much that you would risk falling for it? That's the day I told them I was leaving.

The first poem I wrote about the shooting was vague, almost ecstatic. I submitted it for a workshop with the famous writer sponsored by a literary journal.

I could have tried to write a memoir. But all that I could manage then (and now) was poetry.

Verse lets me throw my voice in a way that prose does not, and I cannot stand to stand too near my voice or it will begin to scream at me.

The poem concluded with a line by Wordsworth: "All which we behold / is full of blessings."

An allusion is a reference to a known idea, in which the idea comes to stand for what the speaker cannot quantify.

One of the other writers in the workshop did not behold the promised blessings. "What about these people, the ones who died?" she said. "You haven't written them."

I think she thought that I was writing secondhand, that I had based the poem on news reports or hearsay. I don't think she realized I was there.

Which is of course my fault, since I wrote it. You cannot craft yourself a guise and then protest when you are not recognized.

I think that I am writing my own absentia, by means of a trial or a distraction.

On the morning of the shooting I meet H. in the hotel lobby. I have a bellboy's cart all loaded up with bankers boxes. My exhibits.

Pages and pages of paper, hundreds of pages. Detailing all the facts I plan to prove.

Exhibits are a proxy for the truth. You look through them to what really happens.

Above the throat of bitterness a mouth erects its language like a bridge.

There are some things I can explain to you and some that I cannot. Some things are found within the public record.

Context, too, is a space available for occupying.

My trial involves a company that makes all kinds of sex toys. Dildos. Vibrators. Pelvises made of flesh-toned rubber. A lurid mouth glowing in the dark, tinted green.

My client, my co-counsel, the other lawyers, the other parties, my bosses, and the judge. All of them are men. How'd you land this case? they ask me, and guffaw.

Will you be using any (dramatic pause . . .) demonstrative exhibits?

This is when I am still married to my first husband. He does not stand for anything not profitable. A woman is an investment and should be made to pay.

The judge was born in Baltimore, where I was also born and where I have always lived. He went to a more prestigious law school and he worked for a more prestigious firm before he took the bench.

We both named our children Ben, though this is not the sort of thing we ever discuss, he and I, at all because he never speaks to me directly.

He only ever speaks to H. I am certain he has forgotten my name completely if he ever even knew it. H. is my proxy, the body that stands in for mine.

One year before the shooting, the judge said controversial things in a trial involving clothes designers. He called the whole proceeding drunken.

"What's a duck shoe?" he asked in open court. Then he wondered if a Jewish person can be a WASP. Perhaps these statements, divorced from context, do not represent the judge's mind.

Or perhaps they do.

He retired several years ago. Now he consults with a Manhattan law firm. I imagine him wearing shoes with laces and sipping bourbon at the Harvard Club.

Like I said, he won't remember me, I'm sure.

After the shooting, he asks H. about the tweeting lawyer, which is me. A synecdoche is a figure of speech in which one part stands for the hole.

One early morning after the shooting and after I have left my husband my friend knocks on the door. She brings inside a twelve-pack of Guinness stout and she drinks all morning, taking breaks to smoke outside and confide in me about the man she fucked the night before.

When I left my husband she decided to start dating. Anyway we call it dating.

We are both going insane in our respective ways, my friend because she is bipolar and has stopped taking her medication, and I because I am, though I don't yet know it, still hiding in a stairwell in a parking garage in Delaware.

H. and I drive through Wilmington in heavy traffic. The courthouse is on King Street. History and all its contexts woven into the seams of what we experience.

Corporate lawyers like the word "acquired"; it sounds more neutral than the truth, which is more like taken. "Purchased" is sometimes like that. So is "fact" or "evidence" or "property" or "sex."

Words smoothly figure an exchange even when the trade is made at gunpoint or by the small print no one reads.

Some language is, in fact, a verbal act. Like the pronouncement that declares two people spouses.

As with a skirt that drapes in such a way as to hide the prize inside. The structure underneath it blocks the wearer's easy passage or escape.

The New Sweden Company men built at what the Lenape people called Paxahakink, and they named the outpost Fort Christina for the Swedish Queen. Now we call it Wilmington.

A nation projects itself across an ocean into space, which is another country, like the past. A vacuum is a necessary fiction.

As are names. As is history. As is every route to trade or fame.

To put it bluntly: every so-called empty space needs filling.

Many Delaware places now are named for Queen Christina: a shopping mall, a hospital, a school district. She was twelve when the ships set sail. A child.

One of the women who will die inside the courthouse lobby is named Christine Belford.

Queen Christina refused to marry. She renounced the throne and retired to the Vatican, where the Pope called her a woman without shame.

My friend is drunk. I would prefer that she go home. It is a little more than one year after the shooting at the courthouse in Wilmington.

I am alone and also not alone because I have made a second body for myself. A way of holding my experience within a fictive space.

An incorporation is a body or a shield, sometimes for profit and sometimes not.

After the shooting I attempt to incorporate, to draw myself together into a new person, someone present to the world. This is a means of avoiding pain, or of doubling it.

A lawyer's job is to draw connections between one fact and another proposition. A lawyer looks to precedent.

A poet's job is to speak connections between things not recognizable as facts but which are true.

As I walk into the courthouse lobby I see, from the periphery, a man turn and run away. He has a large umbrella with him, the old-fashioned kind with a crook in the handle.

This makes me think of the Zapruder film and the Umbrella Man. I don't think of the film at the time. I only think of it now, as I'm writing, because I can infer that the man on the sidewalk saw the gun and ran.

Some people think the Umbrella Man fired a shot at Kennedy. That Oswald did not work alone, that there was a gun concealed inside the umbrella shaft. Thinking of the Zapruder film puts me in mind of Matthew Zapruder, who is a poet.

I read somewhere, once, I think, that he is related to the Zapruder who shot the famous film.

But he is not the famous poet who diagnosed my shock from what I'd written in the poem with the Wordsworth line. I've never met him. He would not know me.

I reach out a tentacle for the name, you see, and pull it in, make it a part of me, move a little farther on.

He has nothing to do with what happened or is happening, but my mind makes these connections

so that it doesn't fall down into the shaft above which it is constantly, precariously, fighting to maintain its balance.

"Zapruder" sounds like the sound of three shots fired in rapid succession.

It is cruel for me to expose a stranger to my violent logic, but cruelty sometimes keeps the drowning mouth afloat.

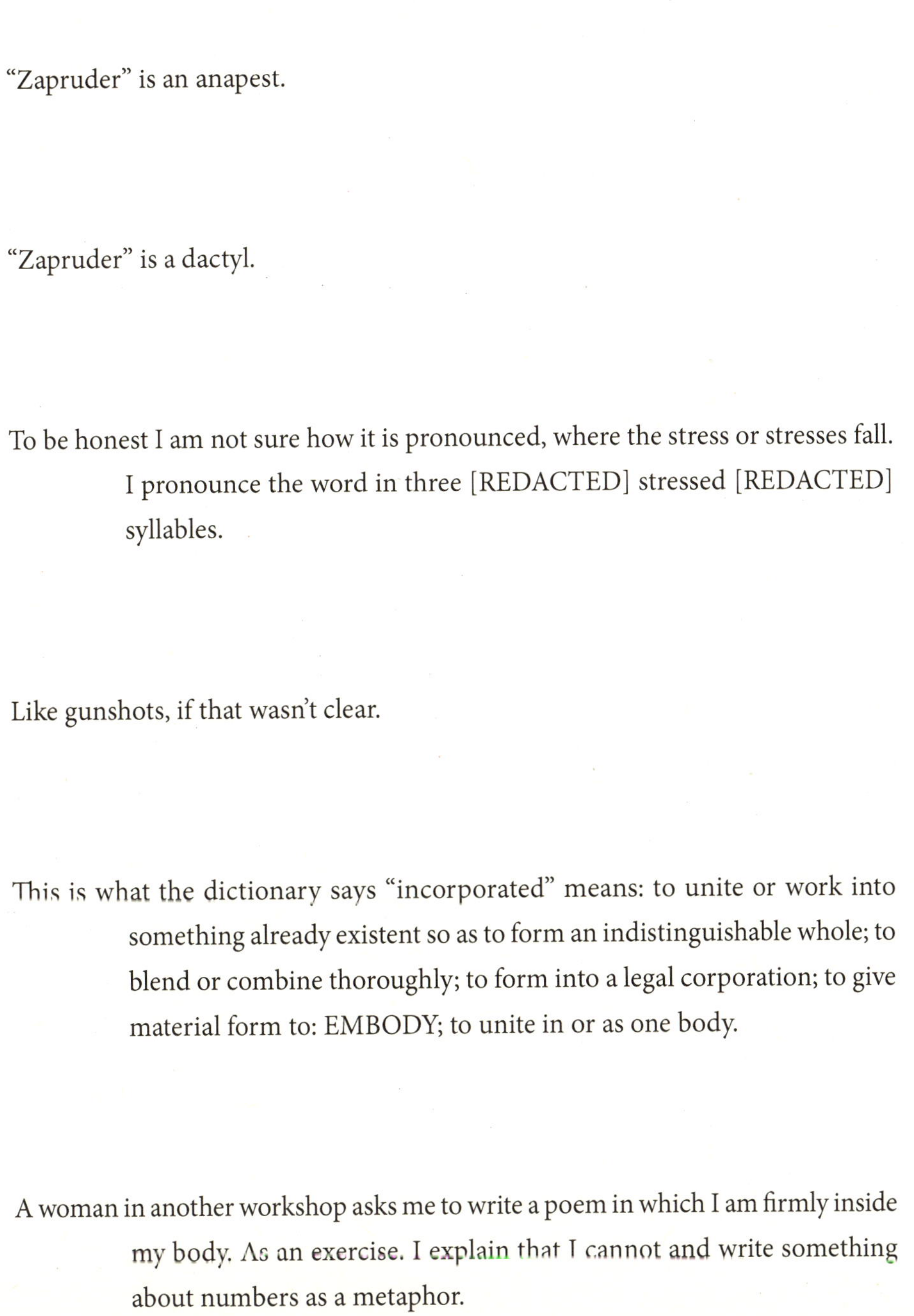

"Zapruder" is an anapest.

"Zapruder" is a dactyl.

To be honest I am not sure how it is pronounced, where the stress or stresses fall. I pronounce the word in three [REDACTED] stressed [REDACTED] syllables.

Like gunshots, if that wasn't clear.

This is what the dictionary says "incorporated" means: to unite or work into something already existent so as to form an indistinguishable whole; to blend or combine thoroughly; to form into a legal corporation; to give material form to: EMBODY; to unite in or as one body.

A woman in another workshop asks me to write a poem in which I am firmly inside my body. As an exercise. I explain that I cannot and write something about numbers as a metaphor.

Numbers are not abstract and they do not admit of pain. They are made of steel and copper.

Math establishes a trajectory from which it never deviates.

After the workshop in which I cannot write from within my body I cry for no less than two (2) hours.

That Valentine's night in 2014, my girlfriend leaves me alone — finally — with my bodies. Text messages roll in, then, one after another after another one:

We will never speak again when this is over and i will get you back for destroying our family and me financally

Fuck you whore

Bye

Eat shit and die whore

I hope you choke on a dick whore

Whore

Whore

Whore

Selfish bitch

Coward

Whore

All hell will now break loose this is now a war

You destroyed me payback time

Bye whore

When I met my husband — let's call him J. — he was very shy. He had never dated anyone before me.

He owned two reclining chairs, a mattress, a weight bench, and a television. He was ten years older. He had no interests other than his work and lifting weights.

These were all what you might call, today, signs of danger, of someone not suited to a gentle life with someone else; but I wanted to be in love with him and so I was.

The first time was in 1995, the year that we got married. I put mushrooms in the ground beef along with other vegetables. J. hates mushrooms but I didn't think that he would notice.

In this assumption I was wrong and this information propels the story forward. The evidence:

Exhibit One: His anger pried a kitchen cabinet door wide open. A pan fell out and clattered on the floor. I cannot remember clearly now. Maybe it was his fist that was loud and not the pan. Maybe it was both.

I don't like to speculate when it comes to faulty memory. It might elicit an objection.

I rarely saw the friend who was visiting with us after that. She absented herself rather than pronounce upon the evidence before her and I cannot blame her.

Exhibit Two: J. accidentally backed the minivan into a concrete pylon in a parking lot and dented the back fender. That was on a Mother's Day. He was so angry at us for what he had done.

Our children had been born by then. Three of them.

A corporation formed for the purpose of committing crime is a conspiracy.

Someone tells me fiction sometimes proceeds in pieces or by tentacles. A tentacle reaches out and pulls in something, another tentacle grabs at something else.

In this way a story moves, by collecting bits of information. Incorporating facts to make a story that holds water.

A story might be nothing more than the odds and ends that come a speaker's way.

Scene in which a woman in a darkened room spins her hair into woolly yarn.

Because I am a lawyer I have access to certain databases. In the first pandemic winter I spend a morning looking up David M., Christine Belford's former husband. I will not reproduce his full name here, or the names of his co-conspirators.

And anyway the story is a matter of the public record.

David M. was tried in federal court with his sister, Amy G., and his mother, Lenore M. Lenore M. died in prison at the age of seventy-one.

I look at Lenore M.'s face. There are photographs of her online. In one of them she wears an Old Navy sweatshirt and sits at a table reading a letter.

She could be a grandmother dyeing Easter eggs or glancing up at the photographer from a game of bridge.

Lenore M. had short gray hair cut in the Jean Seberg style. Looking at her placid smile makes something bitter eat the lining of my throat.

Seberg probably died by her own hand. Federal law enforcement hounded her for years. She hid herself away in France but ultimately could not elude the whispered word campaign intended to extinguish her.

Snuff is snuff. Witnessing means the act cannot be rendered abstract or divorced from what it signifies, establishes through the eyes a space that cannot readily be colonized.

But witnessing means being in the water with the eels, and sometimes it is too difficult. I grasp for what seems solid.

The man who killed Christine and her friend, Beth Mulford, was Thomas M. He was David M.'s father, Christine's former father-in-law.

Beth came to court because Christine was afraid to appear alone. Two women, we have been taught, are less vulnerable than one.

After killing Christine and Beth and wounding two courthouse guards Thomas M. shot himself and was therefore never tried. In this way his body figured as a proxy to the use of David M.

A shareholder who cannot attend a stockholders' meeting but wants to make his wishes known can do so via proxy: this delegates authority to another to cast a vote.

There are many ways to insert a space between the self and what the self desires. And what the self has done.

Several years before the shooting J. was angry because I told him to get out of bed, go outside and play with the children. He stood up. Then he punched me in the jaw.

I am told that sort of punch is called an uppercut. I don't remember what it felt like.

I do remember landing on my hands and knees with my face pressed into the carpet. I remember realizing I had spun around in the air, like an acrobat on a trapeze inside a tent.

The lady and the fulcrum and the canvas sky above her. How light I was, compared to him, compared to everything around me.

When I could I crawled into the bathroom. I tasted metal in my mouth. I locked the door. I put my face into the carpet.

The bathroom rug was still damp from that morning's shower or I cried into it and made it damp. I am not sure. When I thought that J. was no longer standing there, I opened the door and called my brother.

My brother came to the house and the children and I left with him. I didn't know where J. was. I didn't want to spend time packing.

And then, a few days later, we went home. J. promised to be better. I tried to hold on tighter to the bar of my trapeze.

A corporation is like a body. It is like a second body or a shield or a set of clothes. I know that I'm repeating myself. I do this for reassurance, to make certain this is still me speaking.

You don't have to worry about a corporation disappearing. You can always make another one, or breathe money into the one you have.

Scene in which the yarn is spun into a heavy cloth.

I read a Department of Justice press release from 2016. David M., his mother and his sister have been sentenced to spend their lives in prison.

They claim that they had no idea that Thomas M. would kill Christine or her friend Beth or anyone.

It's too much again. I need to think of something else a while. Abstraction, distraction. I know, I've made it obvious.

What I can't remember is the key, I think. What I think I saw but cannot see from either set of eyes. The court requires more evidence to take judicial notice of the truth.

Here I rely upon my training. There are things a juror decides are true without ever having seen them.

It is all too much sometimes but then I get a cup of coffee and it is still too much but I'm effervescent and I sit together.

Distraction is an art like everything else / I do it so it feels real.

This morning I wake up feeling ill, like I have the beginnings of the flu. My legs are heavy. My head aches. I remember that last night my knee was hurting, throbbing really, in the dark until I shifted into another pose.

I wonder if I dreamed that.

Scene in which eels writhe inside a horse's skull.

Yesterday I met with a therapist. My first in several years. She seems nice enough. When I begin to tell her what happened my throat closes up.

"You're just re-traumatizing yourself," she says. This feels strange but also intuitively right. What is happening to me will make itself a new body here, take up residence inside it.

Then I will be free, I think.

Every sentence has an I, at least one, even one left unspoken, for seeing out.

Scene in which the horse's head is bait.

Scene in which the horse's head is a warning.

In Helen Vendler's commentary on "One need not be a Chamber — to be Haunted — " she writes that "startle" is a "cool" word.

"[T]he self-concealing-itself-from-itself is a 'metaphysical' concept rather than a Gothic one."

Since Vendler does not capitalize "metaphysical" I understand her thinking to mean "abstract" or "abstruse," although Donne probably deployed his Metaphysical conceits for purposes not unlike Dickinson's.

Metaphor in criticism is something like jogging in place indoors.

On the same ill-feeling, exhausted morning, S., my second husband, asks me to make breakfast. I decide to make shakshuka. As I slice and chop my hand keeps slipping and I repeatedly dry it on a dishtowel.

Finally I realize that the knife handle is wet.

I am having one of my very tired days. But there is work to be done and my work is speaking, the way the horse's skull returns with eels. I find a lakeside scene on YouTube with an eight-hour run time and let it play.

Power lines run through the scene as they always do.

I swallow swallow swallow all the eels until they are inside my salty naked eye sockets.

Delaware is named for a river named for Baron De La Warr. The title may be of Saxon or Norman origin: *verr*, which means "warrior," or *gara*, meaning "gore."

But the name has come to stand for a person, and the person has come to stand for a body of water, which body has come to stand for earth.

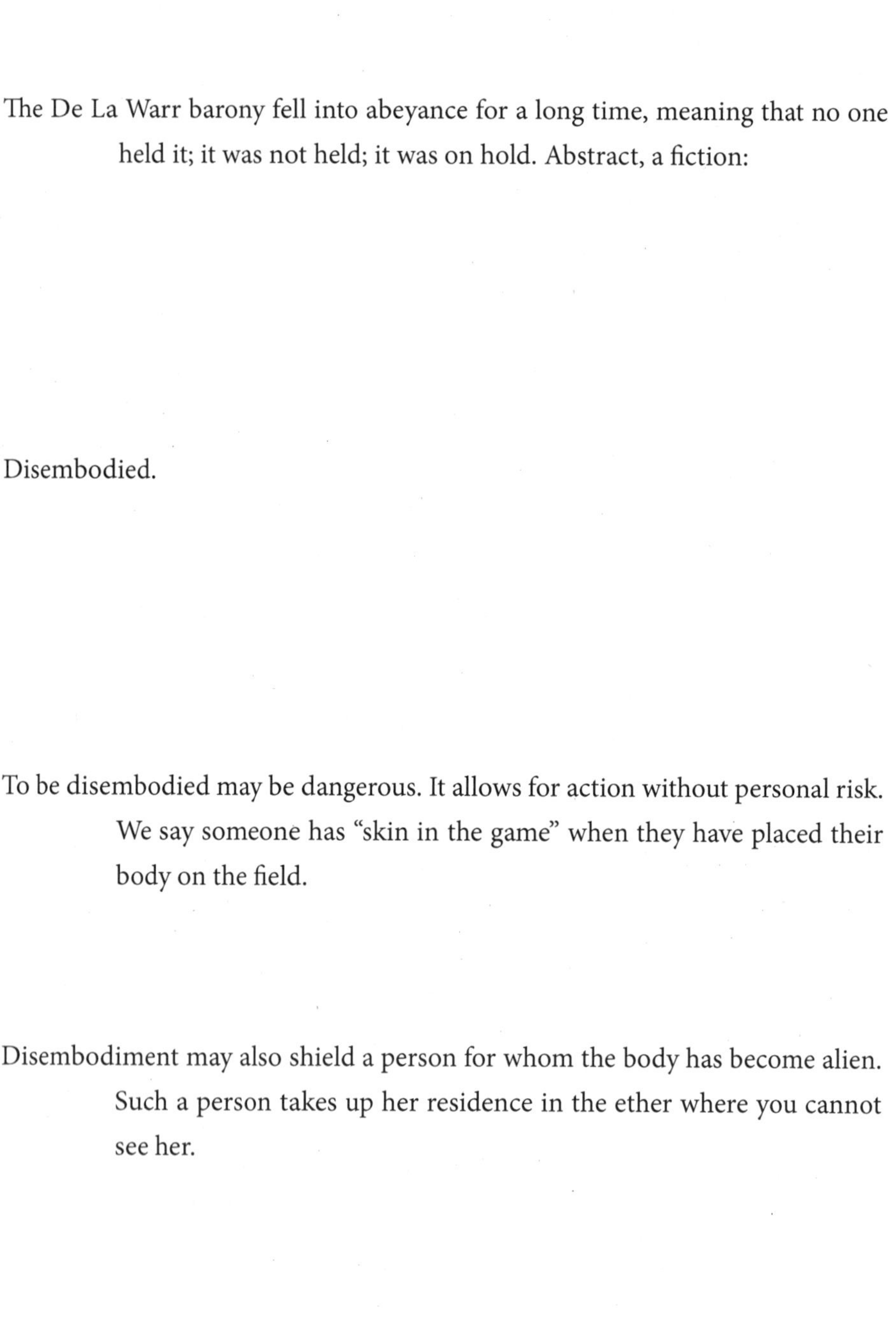

The De La Warr barony fell into abeyance for a long time, meaning that no one held it; it was not held; it was on hold. Abstract, a fiction:

Disembodied.

To be disembodied may be dangerous. It allows for action without personal risk. We say someone has "skin in the game" when they have placed their body on the field.

Disembodiment may also shield a person for whom the body has become alien. Such a person takes up her residence in the ether where you cannot see her.

The De La Warr title is old and venerable, one of the oldest still extant in England. From 1299, when it was first created, to Thomas West, born 1577, for whom the river in the colony was named, through to a child, the current heir apparent, born 2014, one year after the courthouse shooting in the state of Delaware.

Vita Sackville-West was a De La Warr. Her lover thoughtfully critiqued the common law of property in *A Room of One's Own.*

The essay stands for the necessity of physical and figurative space to be occupied by women.

A stanza is a room. You can make it comfortable or you can make it live.

I wish I could stop my mind moving. I wish I could be still.

I move these thoughts into the other body.

Woolen yarns lying on a sandy beach. Woolen yarn spun into a series of interlocking funnels meant for trapping eels.

The DOJ press release and a related court opinion have been open on my laptop for over twenty-four hours. I feel very tired. I decide to go out for a walk.

The windows are still wide open when I return.

More than two days later. Still there. I fix myself a glass of wine.

Why look at awful things if you don't have to? If you can look away.

With eels in the eyes on the sand as they writhe.

Figurative properties are what we define the law by, and the law defines the spaces we inhabit or may not enter.

The law which develops, makes leaps and bounds, via fictions like incorporation. Don't worry about the facts, the law says sometimes, in *obiter dicta* or otherwise in cases. Shade your eyes if they seem too bright.

But I am getting unreasonably far ahead of myself. I am, as they say, at sea.

All Enlightened thinking arises from the law of property: its ownership, its protection, its preservation. Lest someone else appear and claim it for himself.

Doctor Bovary, limp and limpid by the roadside. Professor Tesman, marooned insidc his rationality.

From this insight you may derive certain legal principles. One is self-defense, meaning you may protect your life and the body it resides in. Another is defense of property.

A long, long family line of legal cases concerns the circumstances under which a man can plant a spring gun on his property when he is not at home.

Which is exactly what it sounds like: a shotgun rigged to fire when something springs the trigger. An opened door, a jiggered window.

But I digress. Seeing clearly sometimes is a grief, sometimes a net, one swum into because one is weary in the water and then tangled up in woven panic.

Amy G., Lenore M., and David M. each were charged with cyberstalking and conspiracy.

Cyberstalking is a relatively new crime, one that was being tested in the courts when Christine Belford died. It means using virtual space — the Internet — to harass, stalk or bully someone else.

This space makes a whole new country, a world, a fleet of ships with fictitious names and faces, and they swarm the shoreline with their eely words.

Scene in which a woman's brain is stung by bees and swells, grows pink and angry.

On the morning of February 11, 2013 I step out of the car, carrying a box. At issue is my client's share of a corporation's property.

Clack clack clack of my high heels on the concrete of the parking lot. I walk toward the entrance of the lobby of the Chancery courthouse where equity is done.

From the corner of my eye I catch the movement of an umbrella in a man's hand. The man spins on his heel and runs away from the courthouse. *Away.*

I stop and I think about this. I *think* about what it means that a man has turned to run away on a public sidewalk in an American city in this Age of Aquarius, when guns spring so frequently into public places.

Of what might a man be so afraid in such a place as this? Of what should I be?

And my hand is on the door handle. I think my hand is on the door handle, but it can't be because I am also carrying this heavy box and I need two hands for the box. Maybe I rest one side of the box against my leg so that I can reach for the door handle.

There is a man beside me. Maybe he reaches for the door handle. Beside me with his arm suddenly perpendicular to *terra firma* and I turn

When I was a child the neighborhood boys smacked caps against the concrete curb, pop pop pop

My mother would not allow me to play with caps myself, she felt they were too dangerous but I watched the boys play I watched them

A woman allows a long, long scream

The woman might be me, I'm not sure

Then I am running I am running in my high heeled shoes with my box balanced in front of me it never occurs to me to put the box down the box is suddenly the only tentacle and I need it to be with me or I will be fractured split in two

From somewhere a ship's deck full of gunpowder I think of every film I've ever seen in which shots are fired and I begin to duck behind cars parked along the ramp of the parking garage next door to the courthouse which is the building I have run into brick seems solid and suggests to me I will not disappear if I am inside a brick thing like a building and at the first parked car

there is already a woman hunched there on the ground and she looks at me like there is not enough room here there never is enough room for all of us so I run out and run past several cars and then duck again behind one and crouch there with my box but I realize I am not far enough away from everything that is happening so I run out again still carrying the fucking box and still in the fucking high heeled shoes that I could just kick off couldn't I? why didn't I kick the shoes off and run what sort of woman kicks off her shoes though and I do this repeatedly all the way up the ramp until I am in a stairwell with two other people, a man and a woman, he has his arms around her and we all look at one another but we do not speak and we will never know each other's names

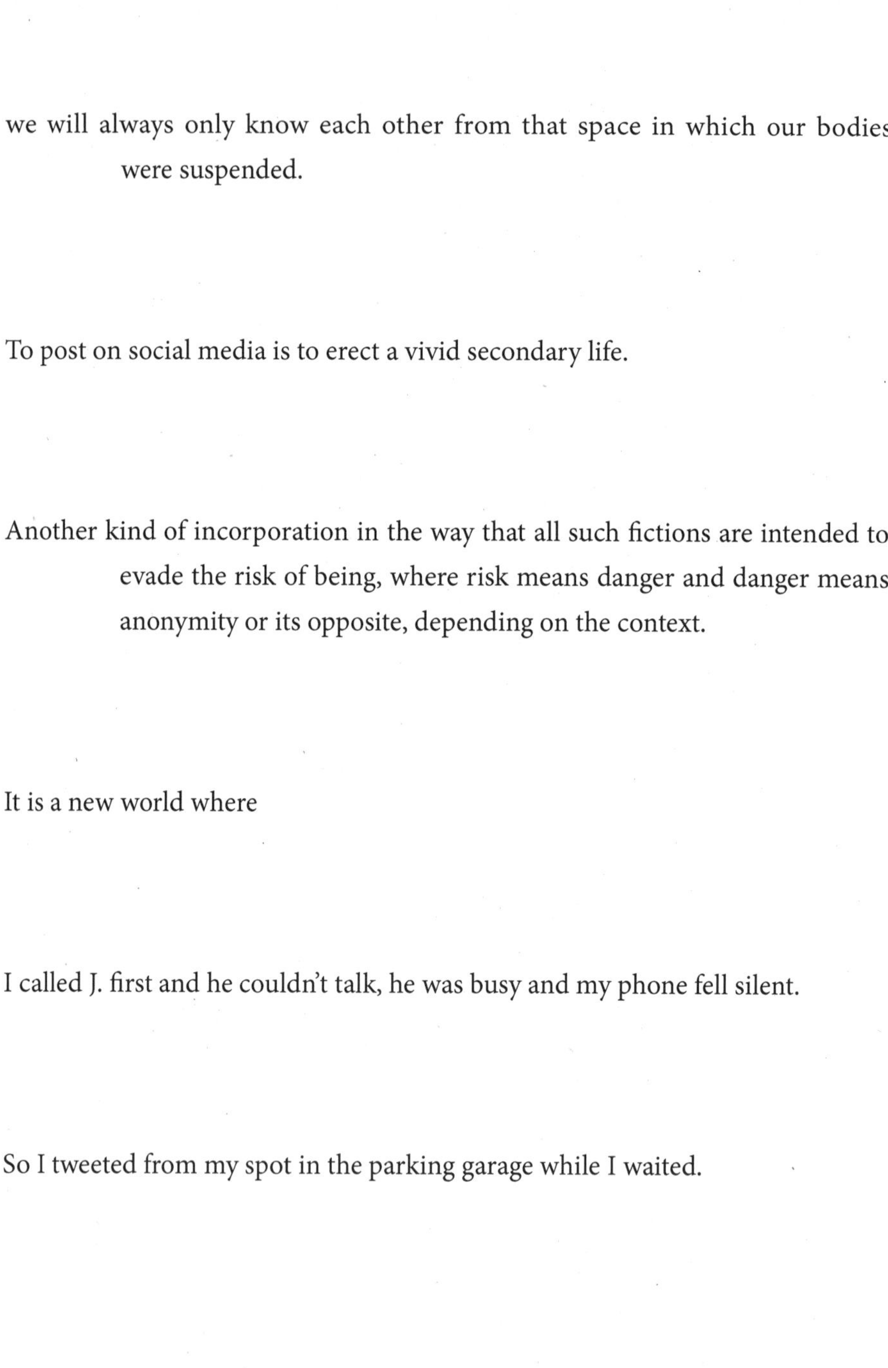

we will always only know each other from that space in which our bodies were suspended.

To post on social media is to erect a vivid secondary life.

Another kind of incorporation in the way that all such fictions are intended to evade the risk of being, where risk means danger and danger means anonymity or its opposite, depending on the context.

It is a new world where

I called J. first and he couldn't talk, he was busy and my phone fell silent.

So I tweeted from my spot in the parking garage while I waited.

I just witnessed my first shooting. DE chancery court lobby. Multiple down. Police here. Where's the #NRA asI'm hiding in parking lot?

8:35 AM — Feb. 11, 2013

I'm okay. Kind of shaken up. Saw shots, people running away, people screaming. 5 people shot

8:48 AM — Feb. 11, 2013

You don't know what you're going to do when something like this happens. I hid in corner shaking like a baby

8:53 AM — Feb. 11, 2013

I am okay. Shaking. You expect to be brave and it turns out you aren't.

9:03 AM — Feb. 11, 2013

A woman was shot in front of my partner. He hid behind our boxes of exhibits on handcart. He says woman will not make it.

9:23 AM — Feb. 11, 2013

This action generates another version of myself in space, a body that is not my body, a narrative meant for public consumption and interpretation. Colonization.

Most of the responses to my tweets are gone now. Accounts have been suspended in the ensuing years or deleted or cleaned up. I blocked the worst of them in the days immediately after and when I was writing this piece I decided against reading them again.

A net lowered into murky water.

There are still these, among many others, a ticker tape of disembodied voices:

could you have prevented if you had a gun?

9:13 PM - Feb 11, 2013

You are in a GUN FREE ZONE they can't help you sorry call copes wait 10 or 20 min.

10:12 AM - Feb 11, 2013

You do have the right to remain silent. Try it for once.

11:26 AM - Feb 11, 2013

Good thing there were GOOD GUYS WITH GUNS to stop the shooter . . .

12:42 PM - 11 Feb 2013

Sad this happened. But blaming guns isn't the answer. Bet if you had the one I keep in my purse you'd have felt a lot safer.

3:13 PM - 11 Feb 2013

please follow back. I am unfollowing people who don't follow back.

4:33 PM - Feb 11, 2013

Several days later, the judge speaks with H. by telephone. He calls me "the tweeting lawyer." H. tells me this and asks me if I am still prepared to try the case.

"We will now explore further ways of reaching our lives, the new / world. My own life, yours; this earth, this moon, this system, / the 'space' we share, which is consciousness."

I tell H. I am. What else is possible?

The next day we are permitted to return, before the court is reopened to the public. We reclaim our boxes of exhibits, and we put on all our evidence.

I avoid the television. I avoid the radio. The trial comes to a close, and I go home.

In 2006, Christine Belford divorced her husband, David M.

One year later David M. and his mother kidnapped David and Christine's children and fled with them to Nicaragua.

When they were found and extradited, David M. pled guilty to the crimes of kidnapping and fraud. He was remitted to the custody of the federal prison system.

But his work did not end with his incarceration.

Christine Belford and David M. had three children. J. and I also have three children.

I am reading the indictment. It is a matter of public record. It is available on the Internet.

The indictment describes a campaign waged for several years by David M., his mother, and his sister, Amy G., to torment Christine on the web and elsewhere.

YouTube, Facebook, other websites, email servers: all kinds of spaces put to use.

The claims were various and without basis. Mostly they alleged that Christine planned to put her children up for sale as part of an amorphous sex trafficking scheme.

Another allegation was that Christine had abused the girls herself; that she was consorting with known sexual offenders; that she had poisoned Lenore M. with some kind of tea.

According to the indictment, the M. family relied on social media to enlist sympathetic people with access to Christine:

> In or around May 2011, [REDACTED] became Facebook "friends" with Christine Belford, and as a result was granted access to Christine Belford's private Facebook profile. [REDACTED] began receiving private updates from Christine Belford about Belford's personal life and the personal lives of Jane Doe 1, 2, 3 and 4. [REDACTED] was a high school friend of DAVID M. and AMY G.
>
> On or about August 18, 2011, [REDACTED], without Christine Belford's knowledge or permission, sent an email to Amy G. attaching a photograph of Jane Doe 1, and stated, "please copy and send to dave! :) love u all!!!! remember shhhhhhhhhhhh!! . . .LOL."
>
> On or about December 12, 2011, [REDACTED] sent emails to THOMAS M. and LENORE M. that contained the real estate listing for Christine Belford's home, which was about to come onto the real estate market. The email contained Christine Belford's seller's disclosure and pictures of various rooms inside her home, including the children's bedrooms.
>
> On or about August 12, 2012, [REDACTED] provided DAVID M. with the username and password to her Facebook account, so that DAVID M. could covertly gain access to Christine Belford's private Facebook profile.

Once out of prison, David M. filed a petition with the family court in Delaware to reduce his monthly child support.

In early February, 2013, David M., his father and his mother left the family home in Texas and drove across the country so that David could appear in family court.

They drove two Hondas. They brought with them weapons, ammunition, restraints, an electric shock device, several gas cans, a shovel, and a cache of photographs.

The photographs depicted Christine and David's children and the home where Christine lived. Christine was absolutely right to be afraid.

Thomas M. left a note behind for Amy G. It read:

ALL MY GUNS TAKE THEM/PROTECT THEM . . . THEY WILL BE YOUR ONLY FREEDOM IN THE COMING YEARS UNDER WHAT WAS ONCE MY GOV'T. WHEN GOV'T TAKES YOUR GRANDCHILDREN AWAY IT CEASES THEN BEING YOUR GOV'T

David M. and Thomas M. entered the courthouse lobby at approximately 7:32 a.m. Thomas carried with him a .45 caliber semi-automatic Glock 21 handgun.

Once inside the lobby, David M. passed through courthouse security while Thomas M. hung back. He could not enter the main lobby because, if he had tried to, his weapon would have been discovered.

And so he waited.

The indictment reads:

At approximately 8:00 a.m., Christine Belford and [REDACTED], a friend who had accompanied Christine Belford to the Courthouse that morning, entered the user lobby of the Courthouse through the revolving door. Within seconds of their entry, THOMAS M. walked directly up to Christine Belford, raised a handgun to her chest, and shot her multiple times, striking her in the chest and arm, and killing her.

Scene in which the woman's brain becomes a swarming hive.

In my body I carry a feeling, and the feeling is in the nature of a cord. And the cord is in the nature of the truth.

I left J. in November, eight months after Christine died on the courthouse lobby floor.

J. was angry. At a hearing he refused to obey the judge and was arrested and then taken into custody. He spent several days in a jail cell muttering and plotting. When he was released the county detailed an officer to my apartment, to watch over me for several days.

I stayed inside my apartment. I stayed inside even after the officer was gone. I have not gone outside, not really, at all since then. I send my second body to do what work is necessary, and I stay inside.

"[A]ll that we behold / is [REDACTED] full of blessings."

I purchase swimming lessons when I am forty-five years old, three years after the courthouse shooting.

It isn't that I need to learn to swim; I learned that as a child.

But I can't put my face in the water anymore, have not been able to for years. I have evolved an awkward style of crawl in which I turn my face from side to side to side, or else I dog-paddle or sidestroke or backstroke.

My instructor wants me to explain how this occurred, and I tell him: when I was ten years old, an ocean wave pulled me under, pressed my face into a vortex of sand and water that suddenly seemed bright, like a camera flash, the old-fashioned kind, a cube, like I was being seared into an image, an image that might substitute itself for me or swallow me alive, and then I felt myself hauled up and returned into the world.

Afterwards I avoided any circumstance in which I might have to look into the water, in case I find myself looking up at me.

Have you ever watched a person drowning? How they turn their head from side to side, a kind of treading water with the eyes.

By the conclusion of my lessons I am able to briefly immerse my face in the water but now several years have passed and

I still avoid the water. I sense nets lurking beneath the surface, things I've woven and things I haven't, and the eels that are caught inside them.

After the shooting I remain in the stairwell until H. texts me. He asks, "Where are you?" And I tell him. He leads me to his car, takes the box from my hands, puts it into the trunk, and then we climb into the seats and wait. After a little while a policeman appears at the passenger-side window and guides us away.

I think to myself, I could stop, I could stop this and sit and read for a while. So I do.

[REDACTED], one of the women referenced in the indictment for assisting the M. family in cyberspace, still maintains a website about Christine. The accusations garish against a yellow background.

The site sets forth claims made originally by affidavit, and from the context the affiant was Lenore M. One bullet-point suggests that Christine planned to sell her daughters for $50,000 each.

Here no one questions why a woman knowingly would threaten such a crime near someone with an axe to grind. But this is not a place for context or nuanced thought or for critique.

Then Lenore M. avers that one day she was changing the girls' bed linens when she found "a rap sheet for a local pedophile" under Christine's bedsheets.

"Could this be the rap sheet of the person who has already agreed to purchase the three children?" the website queries.

This sort of question is, of course, a net, a trap. There are people who will open wide their maws for the hook inside. It is easier to swallow fiction when the mouth and teeth believe the meat is sweet.

It is much more difficult to remain beneath the murky water and swim among the lurking hooks. But if the water will not be empty then something has to live there. This something might be an eel

I am writing all of this longhand in a marble notebook. Later on I will read through it and note where I switched from pen to pencil, for example, or where my handwriting became particularly frenzied.

or it might be a woman and you will have to look closely in order to tell the difference.

The reader will lose access to the context of my composition process. The text alone will offer clues to many things about me and the circumstances of the writing but some things will necessarily remain obscure.

Scene in which the woman wears a band of stinging insects like a crown.

That day the water was both dark and light and I was wrapped up in it, tangled, because the sun penetrated the water through to the sand, and my face was in the sand, pressed hard, and I cannot breathe but for the light. So in time I will go and look for it.

When I am back in the world again I will explain.

Notes

Quoted material not otherwise attributed in the text is from Emily Dickinson's *Master Letters;* William Carlos Williams' *Raleigh Was Right;* Helen Vendler's *Dickinson;* Sylvia Plath's *Lady Lazarus*, and Muriel Rukeyser's *Breaking Open*.

Some of the "scenes" described were inspired by *The Tin Drum* (Volker Schlöndorff, director, 1979).

Acknowledgments

An excerpt from *Bullet Points* appeared in Parhelion Literary Journal.

Thank you to the family, friends, poets and teachers who offered me support, encouragement, and occasional much-deserved redirecting, either as I worked on this manuscript or as I worked my way toward it: Natalie Shapero, Patricia Lockwood, Monica Youn, William Brewer, Cathryn Hankla, Thorpe Moeckel, Karen Bender, Patricia Spears Jones, Liz Poliner, Eve Ettinger, Jonathan Pyner, Kelly Sawin, Matthew Lee, Wayne Sutherland, Colette Fugere. Thank you, Han and Amorak, for shepherding my book into print.

And Stephen, the *only* Stephen, thank you for only everything.

Jennifer A Sutherland is a poet, essayist, attorney and educator from Baltimore, Maryland. She is a graduate of Hollins University (M.F.A.), where she was a teaching fellow; the Catholic University of America, Columbus School of Law (J.D.), where she served as Notes and Comments Editor for the CUA Law Review, and Stevenson University (B.S.). She is an alumna of workshops at Bread Loaf, Tin House, and Kenyon Review. Her creative work has appeared or will appear in *Best New Poets*, *Hopkins Review*, *Appalachian Review*, *Denver Quarterly*, *Hollins Critic*, *I-70 Review*, *Parhelion*, and elsewhere. She is also the author of "Auden and the Unfaltering Hidden Law" and "A Real Danger of Speech in the Social Media Era: Employment Termination," both of which appeared in the *Maryland Bar Journal*, and "The Work for Hire Doctrine Under Community for Creative Non-Violence v. Reid: An Artist's Fair-Weather Friend," which appeared in the *Catholic University Law Review*.

RIVER RIVER BOOKS was founded by Amorak Huey and Han VanderHart in March 2022. Inspired by the idea that you cannot step in the same river twice, two poetry editors join together to publish (at least) two exceptional poetry titles a year.

Catalog

An Eye in Each Square, Lauren Camp, 2023
Bullet Points, Jennifer A Sutherland, 2023
Dear Memphis, Rachel Edelman, 2024
A Geography That Does Not Hurt Us, Carla Sofia Ferreira, 2024